Champions
FOOTBALL

Quotes on Faith,
Guts, Determination,
and Humor

COMPILED BY
Lance Wubbels

"He trains my hands for battle, so that
my arms can bend a bow of bronze."

—2 Samuel 22:35

Champions Speak Out on Football

Copyright © 2007 Lance Wubbels

ISBN 1-932458-28-X

Published by Bronze Bow Publishing, LLC
2600 E. 26th Street, Minneapolis, MN 55406

You can reach us on the Internet at www.bronzebowpublishing.com

Literary development and cover/interior design by Koechel Peterson & Associates, Inc., Minneapolis, Minnesota.

Manufactured in the United States of America

The **Champions Speak Out** *Series*

Champions Speak Out On GOLF

Quotes on Faith, Guts, Determination, and Humor

COMPILED BY
Lance Wubbels

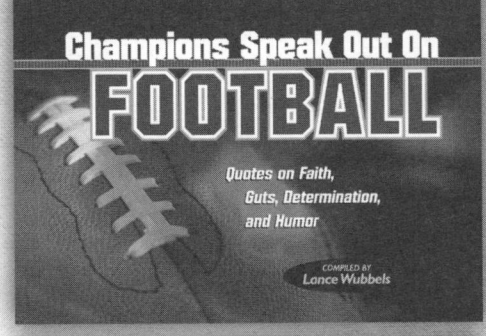

Champions Speak Out On FOOTBALL

Quotes on Faith, Guts, Determination, and Humor

COMPILED BY
Lance Wubbels

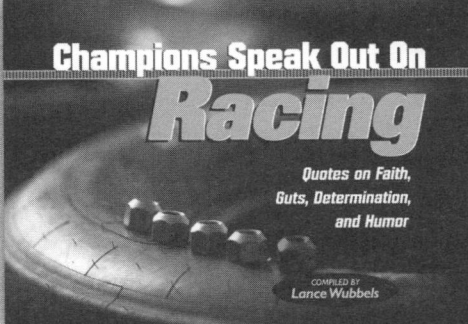

Champions Speak Out On Racing

Quotes on Faith, Guts, Determination, and Humor

COMPILED BY
Lance Wubbels

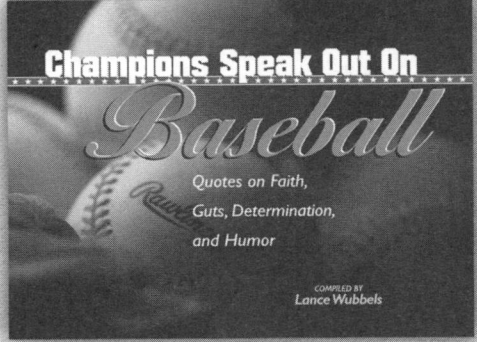

Champions Speak Out On Baseball

Quotes on Faith, Guts, Determination, and Humor

COMPILED BY
Lance Wubbels

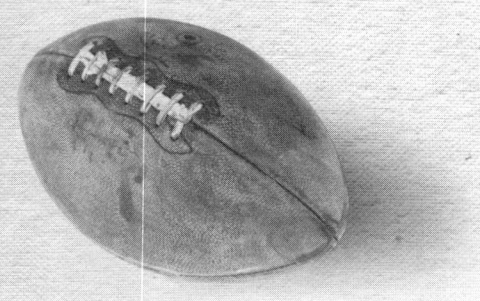

INTRODUCTION

◆ ◆ ◆

For sixteen or more Sundays every fall, we gather by the hundreds of
thousands to be amazed, thrilled, and inspired by the extraordinary feats
of today's professional football teams. The same is true on Friday nights as high
school teams take to the gridiron, and Saturday afternoons when college teams
hold sway over the masses in stadiums across this great land. But it all starts when

a child tosses his first wobbly pass or makes a fingertip catch of a leather football. With that ball we catch something of the dream to excel in the game of life.

From Rockne, Heisman, Lombardi, Wilkinson, and Robinson to Unitas, Butkas, Brown, Nitschke, Namath, and Sayers to Lambert, Singletary, Payton, Marino, Montana, Rice, and Smith, football has charmed and dominated the American landscape in a way that its father, Walter Camp, never envisioned in the late 1800s. All across America at every age level we meet at the line of scrimmage to battle and overcome the odds. And when we're too old to play on the field, there are fantasy leagues to keep those aspirations alive.

There is nothing quite like the game of football for its practical application to living our lives. It is a battlefield that mimics life to the maximum with its demands for strategy, leadership, grit, determination, perseverance, overcoming adversity and injury, and winning in the trenches. Football is a game where inches determine the difference between victory and defeat. It is a game of execution and timing and leaving everything on the field at the end of the day.

The game's greatest players and coaches have much to teach us about how we should approach life. If we're wise, we'll read their unforgettable words and draw from their wisdom and insight.

◆ ◆ ◆

"A winner never quits,
and a quitter never wins."

KNUTE ROCKNE

"When you're a little kid, you dream about holding the trophy up after throwing the winning touchdown or scoring the winning touchdown. This is what it's all about. It's what we've played for all these years."

KURT WARNER

◆ ◆ ◆

"God doesn't want your ability— He wants your availability."

BOBBY BOWDEN

◆ ◆ ◆

"If you want to get better, work a little harder."

JERRY RICE

"Good things happen to those who hustle."

CHUCK NOLL

◆ ◆ ◆

"If you're going to be a champion, you must be willing to pay a greater price than your opponent."

BUD WILKINSON

◆ ◆ ◆

"The key to my success? Understanding that there's no free lunch."

LOU HOLTZ

"Guts win more games than ability."

BOB ZUPPKE

"If you don't give that extra effort and make the sacrifices, if you don't work hard at it, you won't make it because the competition is too great."

OTTO GRAHAM

◆ ◆ ◆

"You get out of life, and out of football, exactly what you put into it. When a person realizes this and acts accordingly, he is sure to succeed."

BART STARR

◆ ◆ ◆

"For when that One Great Scorer comes to mark against your name, He writes—not that you won or lost—but how you played the game."

GRANTLAND RICE

"Discover the talent that God has given you.
Then go out and make the most of it."

STEVE SPURRIER

◆ ◆ ◆

"Success is knowing God. In football, the world defines success as being the best at your position, having a bunch of endorsements, having a big contract. But that's not true success. Having those things doesn't fulfill anyone. The Bible says that success is having a relationship with Jesus Christ."

MARK BRUNELL

"Success is never final.
Failure is never fatal."

JOE PATERNO

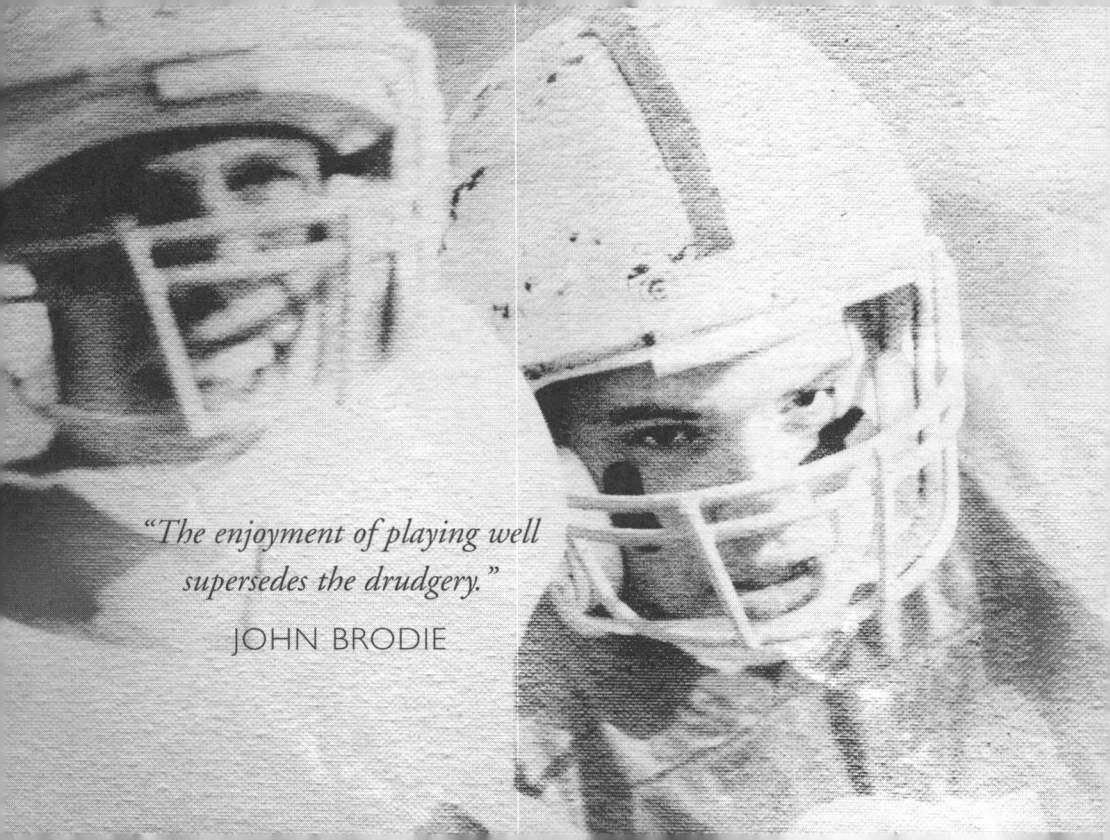

*"The enjoyment of playing well
supersedes the drudgery."*

JOHN BRODIE

"Always remember that Goliath was
a 40-point favorite over little David."

SHUG JORDAN

◆ ◆ ◆

*"Winning is why we do what we do. We play the game to win.
We play the game to finish what we've started."*

AENEAS WILLIAMS

◆ ◆ ◆

"The past is history. Make the present good,
and the past will take care of itself."

KNUTE ROCKNE

"I don't know how I could have ever been effective if I didn't know the Lord. That gave me an opportunity to be free and play the game not for money or accolades or yelling fans but to give the glory back to the Lord."

MIKE SINGLETARY

◆ ◆ ◆

"Either love your players or get out of coaching."

BOBBY DODD

◆ ◆ ◆

"The more successful you become, the longer the yardstick people use to measure you by."

TOM LANDRY

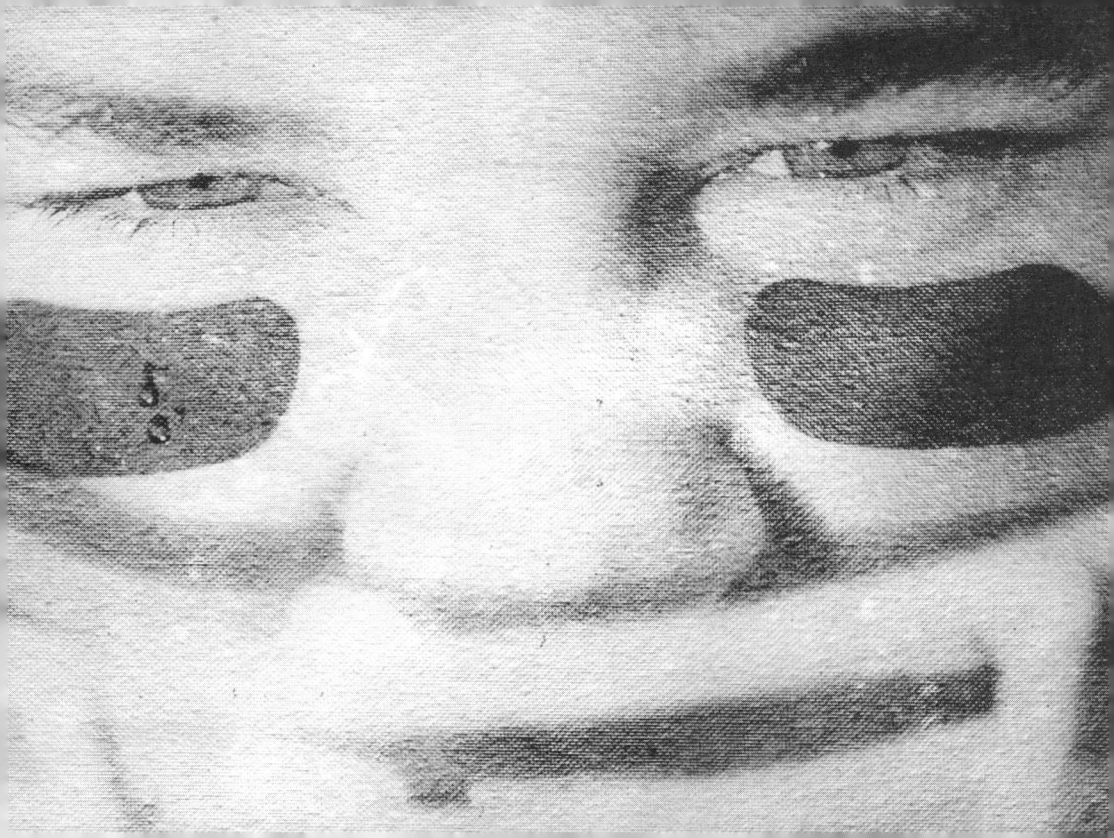

"The harder you work,
the harder it is to surrender."

VINCE LOMBARDI

"Having a heart for Christ makes you have the heart of a champion, because you're going out and doing your all for Him. When you are devoted to that, it doesn't matter whether you win or lose. That's not what makes a champion. What defines a champion is having that desire to work and give your all and have no fear and have no regrets about what you left behind."

JOHN MICHELS

◆ ◆ ◆

"There are no office hours for champions."

PAUL DITZEL

"Money—can this make you happy? No. Superbowls—did that make you happy? No. Do cars make you happy? No. Has jewelry made you happy? No. Have women made you happy? No. So what can give you the final peace that you've been missing, that you've been grasping for all your life? It's only the peace of God, and that's free. It doesn't cost you anything."

DEION SANDERS

◆ ◆ ◆

"Character is determined in the second half."

BERNIE CASEY

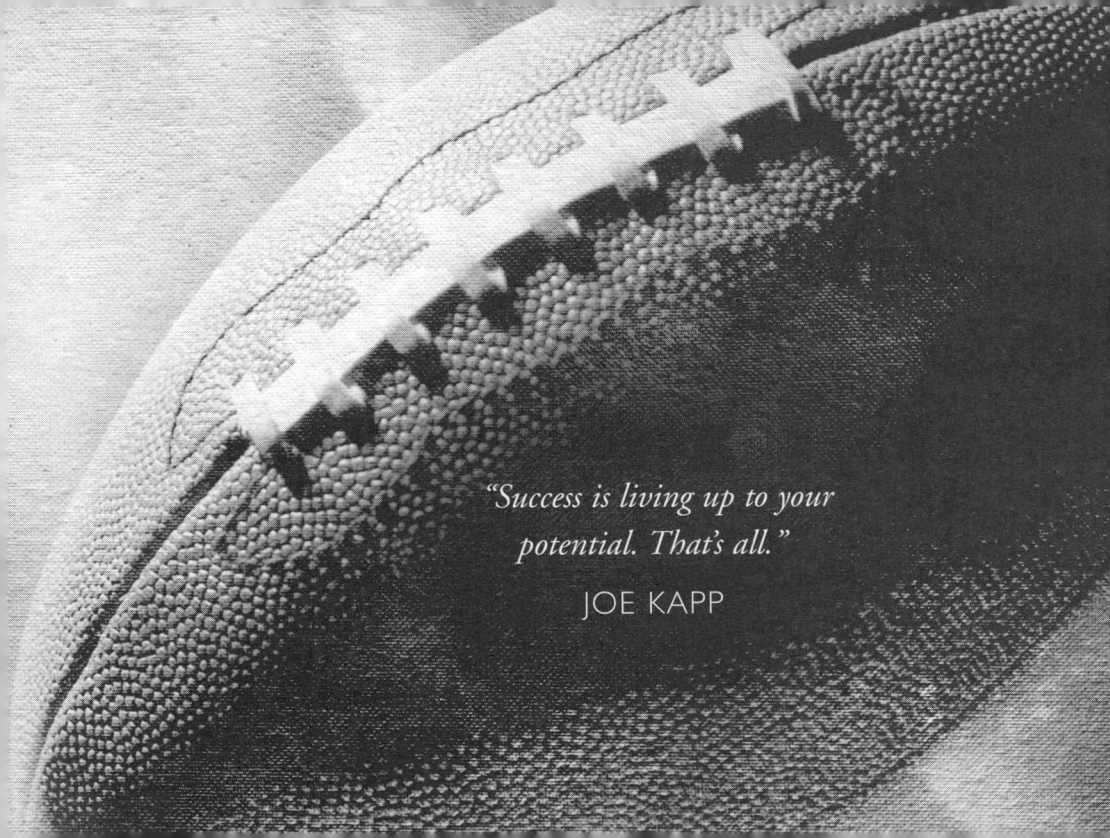

"Success is living up to your potential. That's all."

JOE KAPP

I don't believe in miracles.
I believe in character."
PAT DYE

"When you win, you're an old pro.
When you lose, you're an old man."

CHARLIE CONERLY

◆ ◆

"All that I accomplish is not because of me.
It's because of God and the offensive line."

WALTER PAYTON

◆ ◆

"Confidence comes from hours and days and weeks
and years of constant work and dedication."

ROGER STAUBACH

"Try not to do too many things at once. Know what you want, the number-one thing today and tomorrow. Persevere and get it done."

GEORGE ALLEN

◆ ◆ ◆

"The only problem with doing the impossible is that everybody expects you to duplicate the impossible."

JOHN McKAY

◆ ◆ ◆

"Everyone has some fear. A man who has no fear belongs in a mental institution. Or on special teams."

WALT MICHAELS

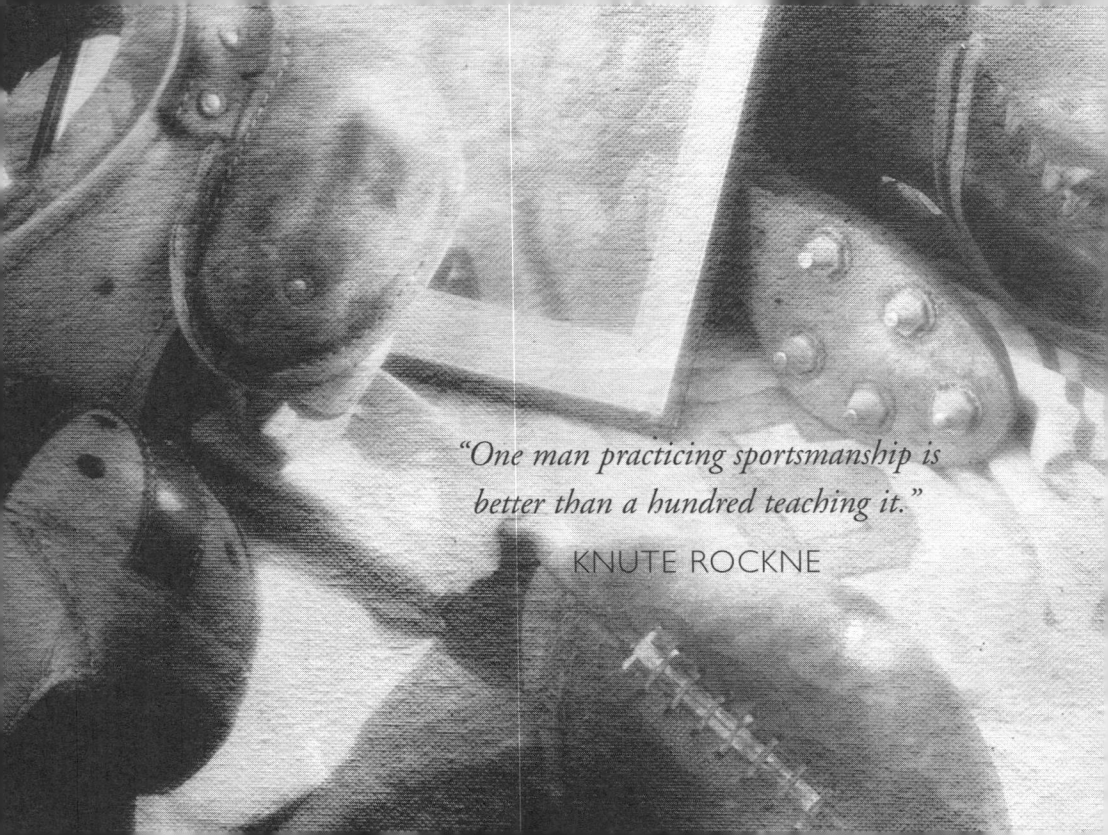

"One man practicing sportsmanship is better than a hundred teaching it."

KNUTE ROCKNE

"Everyone who ever picks up a football dreams about playing in the big game."

JACKIE HARRIS

◆ ◆ ◆

"My athletes are always willing to accept my advice as long as it doesn't conflict with their view."

LOU HOLTZ

◆ ◆ ◆

"Nobody becomes great without self-doubt. But you can't let it consume you."

JOHN McKAY

*"Experience is not what happens to a man.
It's what a man does with what happens to him."*

CHUCK KNOX

◆ ◆ ◆

"The spirit, the will to win, and the will to excel—
these are the things that endure."

VINCE LOMBARDI

◆ ◆ ◆

*"Marcus Allen carries so many tacklers with him,
he's listed in the Yellow Pages under Public Transportation."*

BOB HOPE

"Football is a wonderful way to get rid of aggressions without going to jail for it."

HEYWOOD HALE BROUN

◆ ◆ ◆

You have to have perseverance. Sometimes things will go wrong for three quarters, but if you persevere it's possible that in the fourth quarter things will change, things will turn around for you, and you'll have a victory.

KYLE BRADY

◆ ◆ ◆

"No coach sure of himself and his team constantly bawls out the athletes."

JOCK SUTHERLAND

"I don't hire anybody not brighter than I am.
If they're not brighter than I am, I don't need them."

BEAR BRYANT

"Leadership, like coaching, is fighting for the hearts and
souls of men and getting them to believe in you."

EDDIE ROBINSON

"The Rose Bowl is the only bowl I've ever seen
that I didn't have to clean."

ERMA BOMBECK

"Nothing is work unless you'd rather be doing something else."

GEORGE HALAS

"The real make of a man is how he treats people who can never do anything for him."

DARRELL ROYAL

"Early in my career, I didn't put nearly as much time and effort into my work as I do now. Getting cut really made me work hard. I expect a lot out of myself. I know what I'm capable of doing. That's the reason why I get up at six in the morning and work out. Success is based upon getting the most out of what God has given you."

CRIS CARTER

◆ ◆ ◆

"If you cheat on the practice field, you'll cheat in the game. And if you cheat in the game, you'll cheat the rest of your life."

VINCE LOMBARDI

"To me, football is a context in embarrassments. The quarterback is out there to embarrass me in front of my friends, my teammates, my coach, my wife, and my three boys. The quarterback doesn't leave me any choice. I've got to embarrass him instead."

ALEX KARRAS

———◆ ◆ ◆———

"Always spread out the credit, and never point fingers."

KEN ANDERSON

———◆ ◆ ◆———

"A good coach needs three things: a patient wife, a loyal dog, and a great quarterback—not necessarily in that order."

BUD GRANT

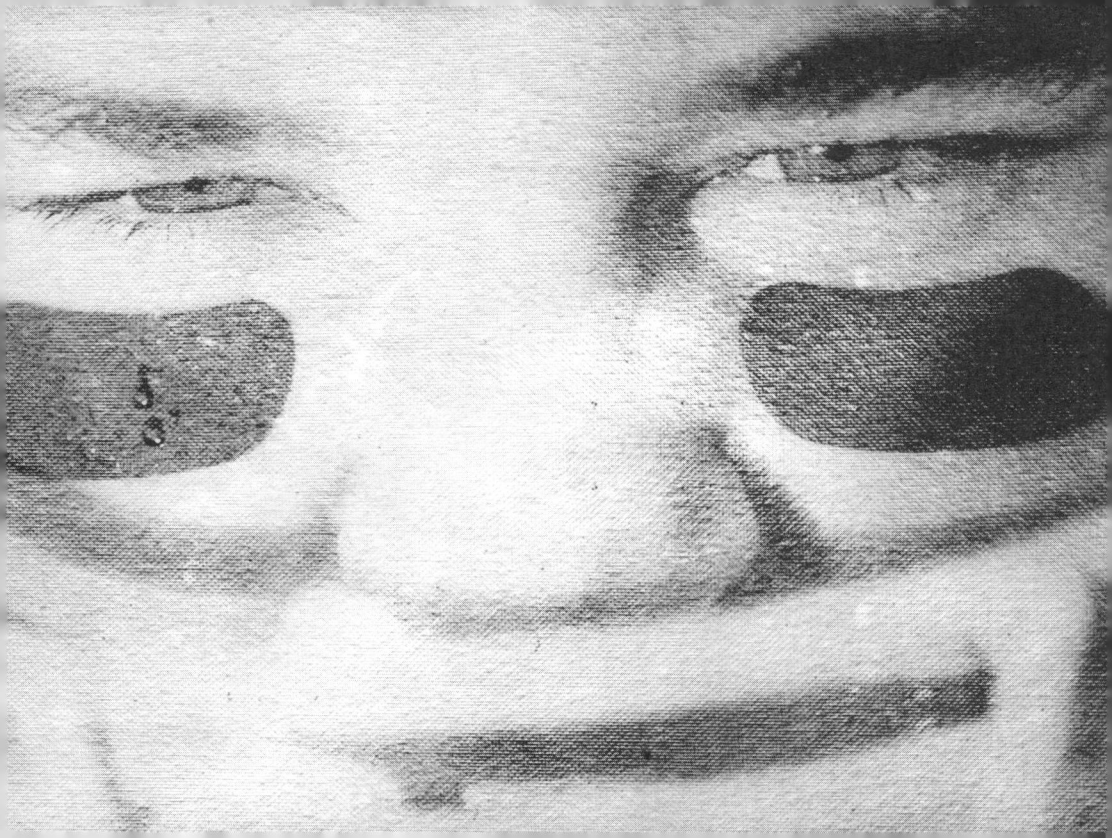

"There are a thousand reasons for failure but not a single excuse."

MIKE REID

*"Coaches who can outline plays are a dime a dozen.
The ones who win get inside their players and motivate them."*

VINCE LOMBARDI

◆ ◆ ◆

"A genius in the NFL is a guy who won last week."

JOHN McKAY

◆ ◆ ◆

*"Coaches have to watch for what they don't want to see
and to listen to what they don't want to hear."*

JOHN MADDEN

"I've got to go out and be motivated.
I've got to work harder than ever.
Because this is precious.
What God has given me is precious."

IRVING FRYAR

◆ ◆ ◆

*"Apart from an innate grasp of tactical concepts, a
great coach must possess the essential attributes of
leadership which mold men into a cohesive, fighting
team with an invincible will to victory."*

GENERAL DOUGLAS MacARTHUR

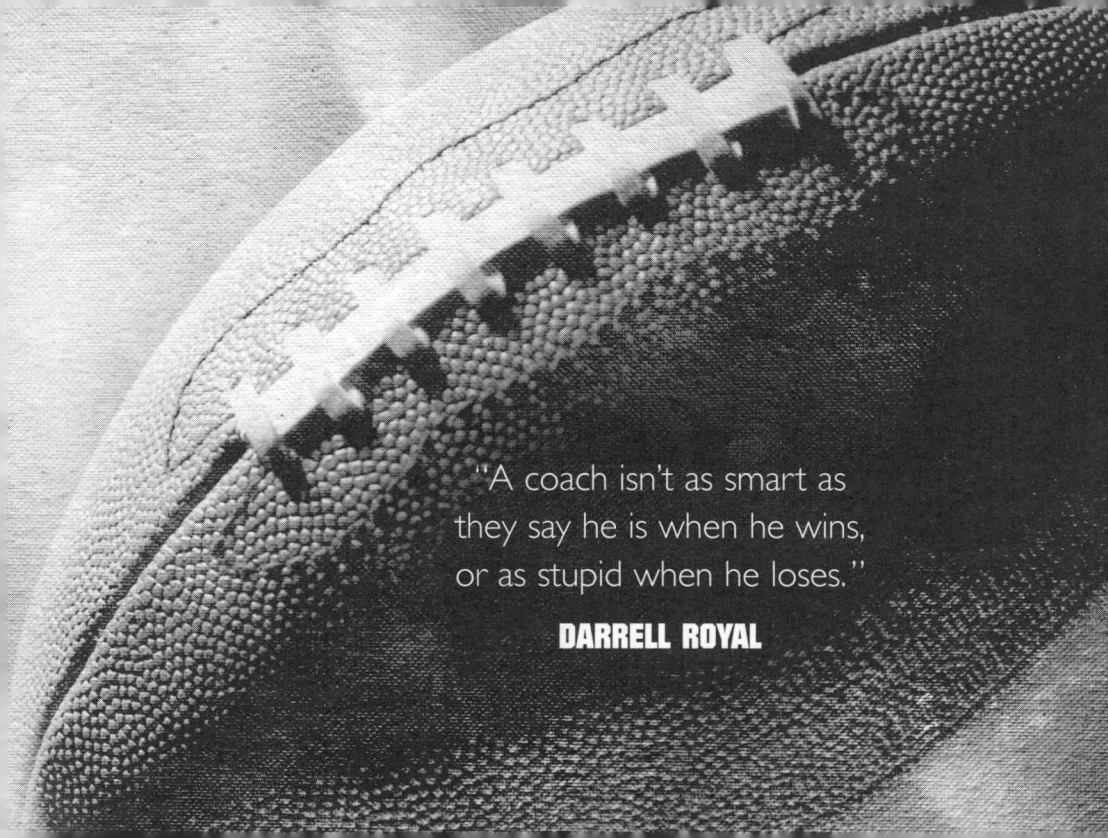

"A coach isn't as smart as they say he is when he wins, or as stupid when he loses."

DARRELL ROYAL

"The game changes, but the real players don't."

HANK STRAM

"When you win, nothing hurts."

JOE NAMATH

◆ ◆

"A spoonful of humor makes the message go down easier."

FRANK LEAHY

◆ ◆

"When it comes to celebrating,
act like you've been there before."

TERRY BOWDEN

"When I got into the coaching business, I knew I was getting into a high-risk, high-profile profession, so I adopted a philosophy I've never wavered from. Yesterday is a canceled check, today is cash on the line, tomorrow is a promissory note."

HANK STRAM

◆ ◆ ◆

"Poise means never fighting yourself."

BOB TYLER

◆ ◆ ◆

"Being respected is more important than being popular."

LOU HOLTZ

"When Jim Thorpe hit me, it felt like a locomotive followed by a ten-ton truck rambling over the remains."

KNUTE ROCKNE

◆ ◆ ◆

"Now that I'm retired, I want to say that all defensive linemen are sissies."

DAN FOUTS

◆ ◆ ◆

"Forget the past—the future will give you plenty to worry about."

GEORGE ALLEN

"We don't care how big or strong opponents are as long as they are human."

BOB ZUPPKE

◆ ◆ ◆

"John Elway is an immediate cure for coach's burnout."

JOHN MADDEN

◆ ◆ ◆

"Winning is a habit. Unfortunately, so is losing."

VINCE LOMBARDI

"Always have a plan
and believe in it."

CHUCK KNOX

"You can learn a lot from adversity. Adversity can make you stronger. It can bring a team together or it can divide a team."

MARK BRUNELL

◆ ◆ ◆

"John Elway is the master of the inconceivable pass thrown to the unreachable spot."

PAT SUMMERALL

◆ ◆ ◆

"There are no shortcuts in life—only those we imagine."

FRANK LEAHY

"Football features two of the worst aspects of American life—violence and committee meetings."

GEORGE WILL

———————— ◆ ◆ ◆ ————————

"I believe that almost every ball is catchable. A lot of the great catches I've made, I never thought I'd catch them. What I try to do is stop the ball—the point of it. Sometimes there's kind of a sweet spot. If I'm able to grab that spot on the football, I feel I can control it or bring it in."

CRIS CARTER

———————— ◆ ◆ ◆ ————————

"Coach a boy as if he were your own son."

EDDIE ROBINSON

"It's not whether you get knocked down,
it's whether you get up."

VINCE LOMBARDI

"My mother died of cancer in 1981, and my father died of a heart attack in 1982. I had focused on setting my goals and everything to please them. My brother Sam taught me one thing. He said, 'Live by this. Be a leader. Do well in school. Set your goals. Always do what's right, and not what's wrong, and you'll be successful.' That's the way I've lived my life."

RANDALL CUNNINGHAM

◆ ◆ ◆

"My coaching philosophy? Determine your players' talents and give them every weapon to get the most from those talents."

DON SHULA

"Commitment is a way of life. There are no shortcuts to success. You can't cut corners. You have to have that discipline to go the extra mile, to pay the price. That means doing the weights, the running, sitting in 105-degree temperatures and sweating until you think you can't go anymore, but then going that extra mile. It's the same sort of commitment that it takes to do what's right. A lot of times what's right is not always the easiest path to take. And that's where that discipline and commitment come in to help you choose a path that is the correct path."

CHAD HENNINGS

◆ ◆ ◆

"I can't believe God put us on this earth to be ordinary."

LOU HOLTZ

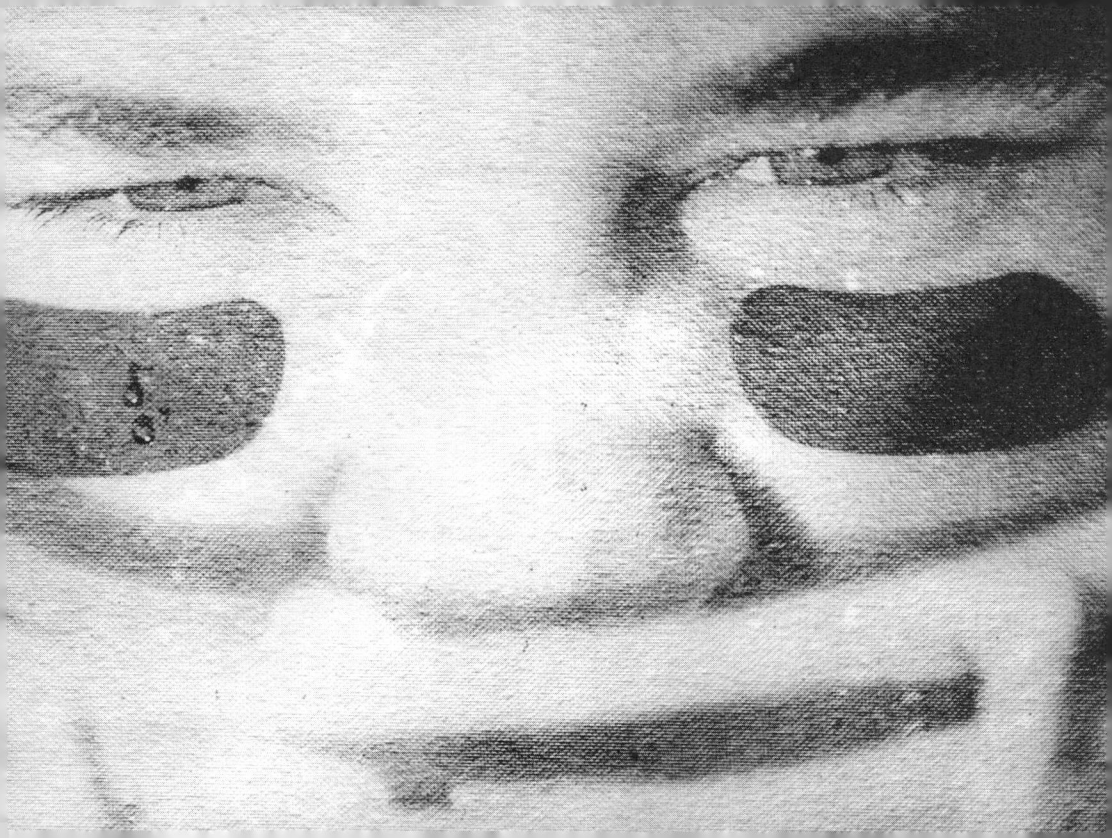

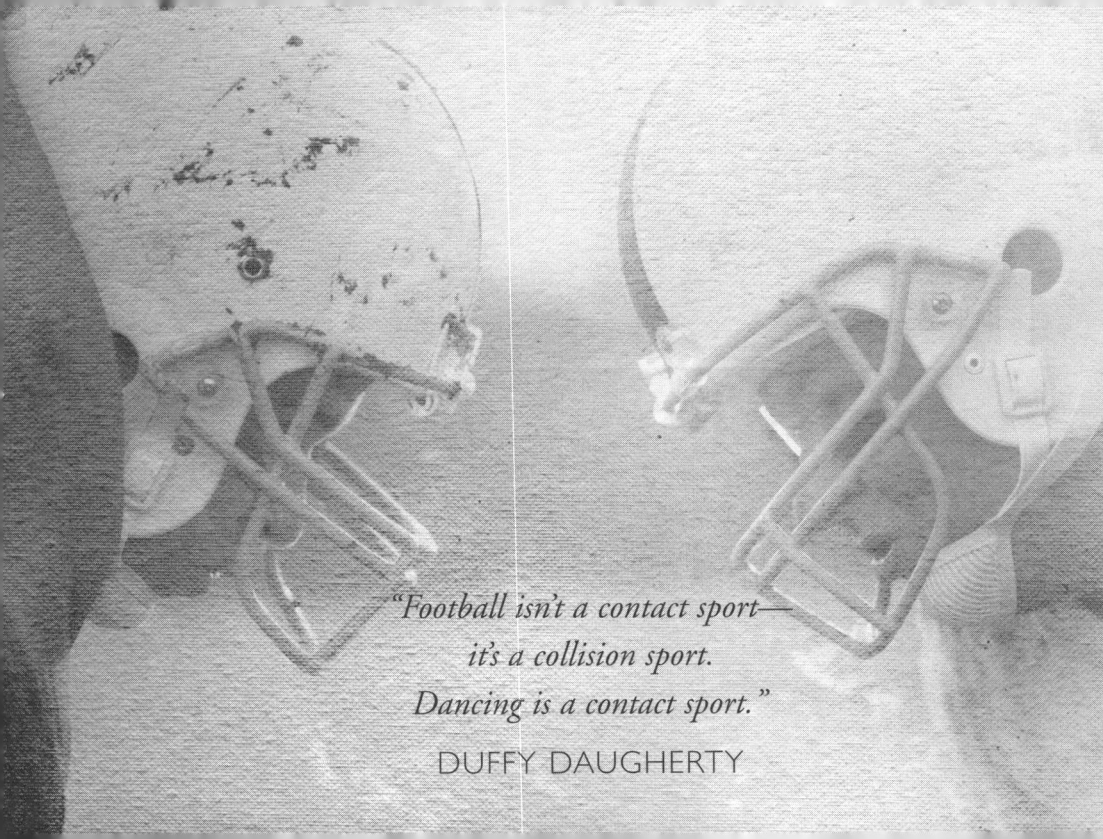

*"Football isn't a contact sport—
it's a collision sport.
Dancing is a contact sport."*

DUFFY DAUGHERTY

"When I first played middle linebacker in the seventh grade, my coach told me, 'You'll have to be the roughest guy on the field, but still be responsible for all the other guys on the field.' From then on, to me the role of middle linebacker was to assume leadership on the field. When I left the field, I wanted everything to be left on the field."

MIKE SINGLETARY

◆ ◆ ◆

"One thing never changes: the team that controls the line of scrimmage wins the game."

BUD WILKINSON

"When I'm out there on the field, I'm out there to do my job. Just because you're a Christian, it doesn't mean you can't line up out there and try to knock some guy into next week."

GREG LLOYD

— ◆ ◆ ◆ —

"You can learn more character on the two-yard line than you can anywhere in life."

PAUL DIETZEL

*"The first thing any coaching staff must do is weed out selfishness.
No program can be successful with players
who put themselves ahead of the team."*

JOHNNY MAJORS

◆ ◆ ◆

"Fellows, you have 60 minutes for redemption
and a lifetime for regrets."

FRITZ CRISLER

◆ ◆ ◆

"Don't talk too much or too soon."

BEAR BRYANT

"I played six positions in ten years and did none of them justice. So I decided to quit while I was still on the bottom."

ALEX HAWKINS

◆ ◆ ◆

"I want to rock his world, but I never want him to get hurt. Coming from the blind side, you just de-cleat him, which's what you just always dream of. Hitting somebody so hard that you knock the wind out of them or their helmet flies off."

BRYCE PAUP

"All quitters
are good losers."

BOB ZUPPKE

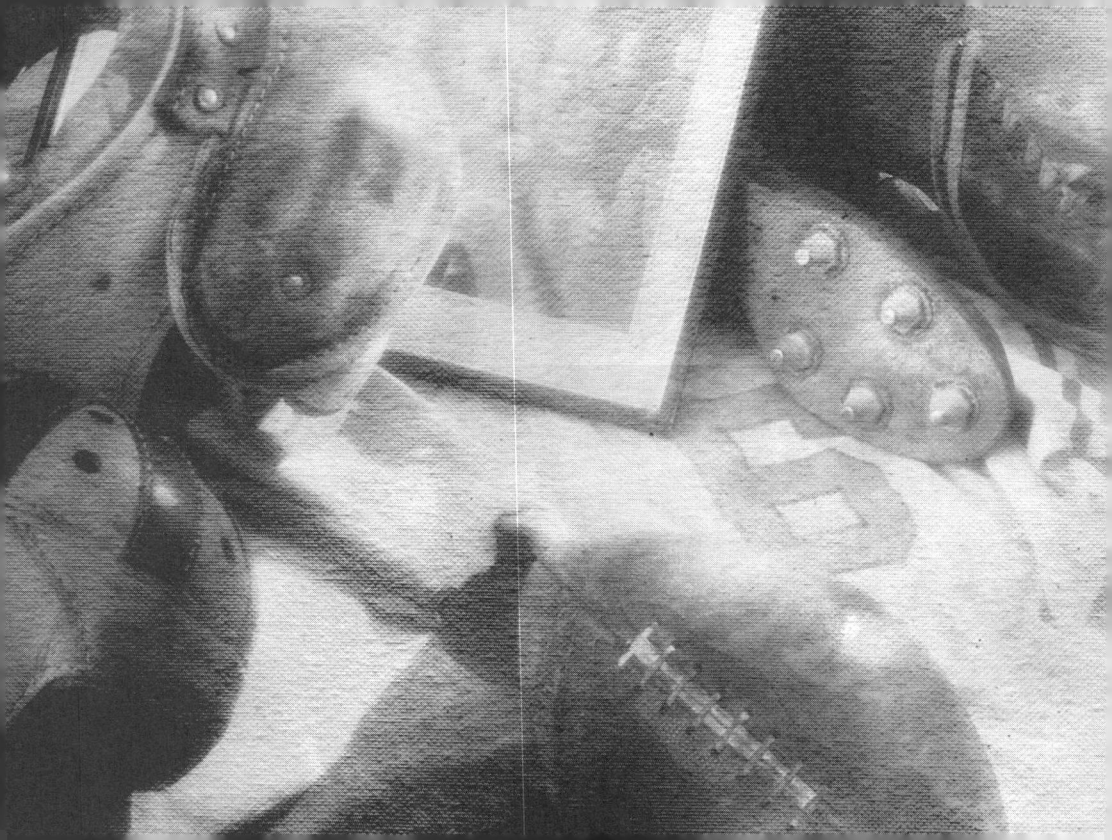

"The man who complains about the way the ball bounces is likely the one who dropped it."

LOU HOLTZ

◆ ◆ ◆

"First become a winner in life. Then it's easier to become a winner on the field."

TOM LANDRY

◆ ◆ ◆

"Work hard, stay positive, and get up early. It's the best part of the day."

GEORGE ALLEN

"We're the tempo-setters. No matter how big the game is, you can't go out there and wish for good things. You have to go out there and make it happen. I play all my games hard and physical. I just can't wait to make a big play and create some havoc."

JESSE TUGGLE

◆ ◆ ◆

"Football is blocking and tackling. Everything else is mythology."

VINCE LOMBARDI

"Leadership must be demonstrated, not announced."

FRAN TARKENTON

"The future is now."

GEORGE ALLEN

"There are two ways to build a team. You either get better players or get the players you've got to play better."

BUM PHILLIPS

◆ ◆ ◆

"Hitting is the one thing that wins games. You make mistakes, but if you're hitting, things will eventually go your way."

JOHN MACKEY

◆ ◆ ◆

"Good fellows are a dime a dozen, but an aggressive leader is priceless."

RED BLAIK

"Not everybody is going to win. There's going to be a loser. The question is how are you going to come back if you lose? Are you going to be negative and start complaining? Or are you going to take it to another level and anticipate the next game, turning it into a positive?"

JIM SCHWARTZ

◆ ◆ ◆

"In the end, the game comes down to one thing: man against man. May the best man win."

SAM HUFF

"You never know how a horse will pull until you hook him to a heavy load."

BEAR BRYANT

"A receiver should run
with his head."

BERNIE CASEY

"Be consistent, play aggressive, play fast, and be disciplined."

CORNELIUS BENNETT

◆ ◆ ◆

"Discipline, with team togetherness, wins football games."

JOHNNY VAUGHT

◆ ◆ ◆

"Success is what you do with your ability. It's how you use your talent."

GEORGE ALLEN

"Whoever I line up on, I tell him it's not going to be an easy day. I'm letting him know right now, because they're only going to be as good as I let them be. You win some and you lose some, but if you don't go into a game believing you're going to win, you already lost before you got out there on the football field."

RAY BUCHANAN

◆ ◆ ◆

"Football is a game played with arms and legs and shoulders, but mainly from the neck up."

KNUTE ROCKNE

◆ ◆ ◆

"Find out what the other team wants to do. Then take it away from them."

GEORGE HALAS

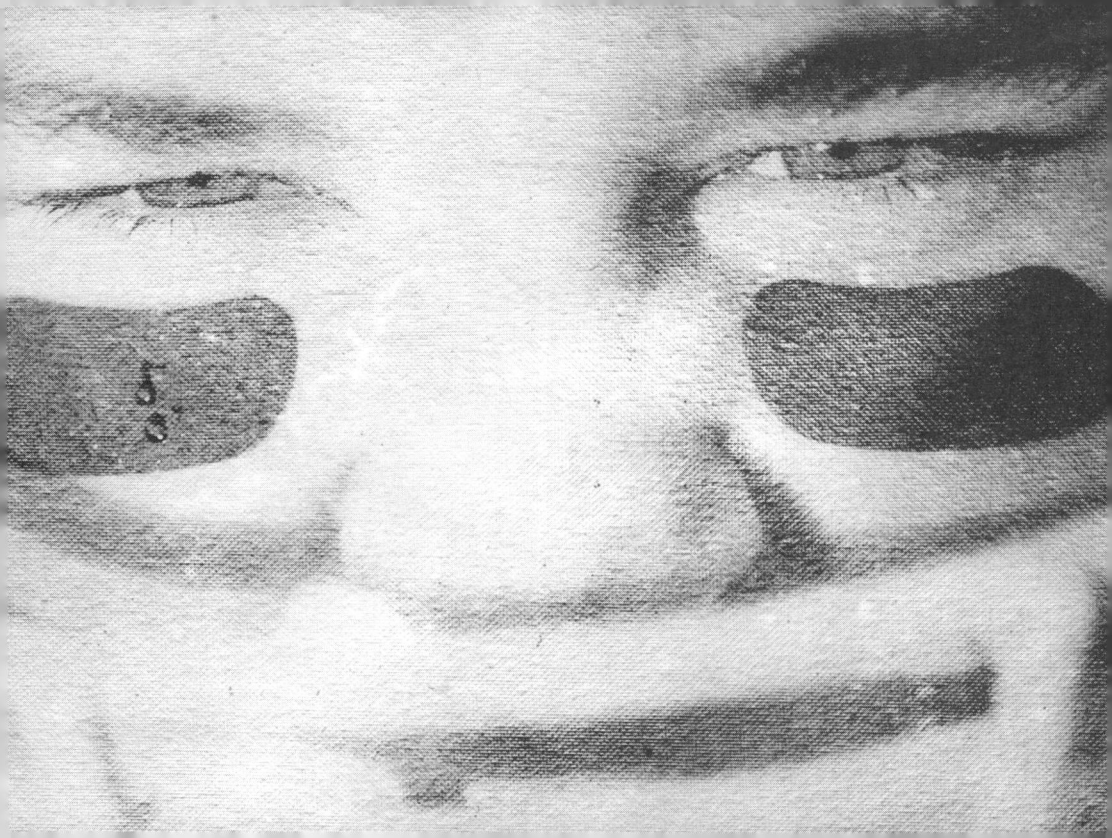

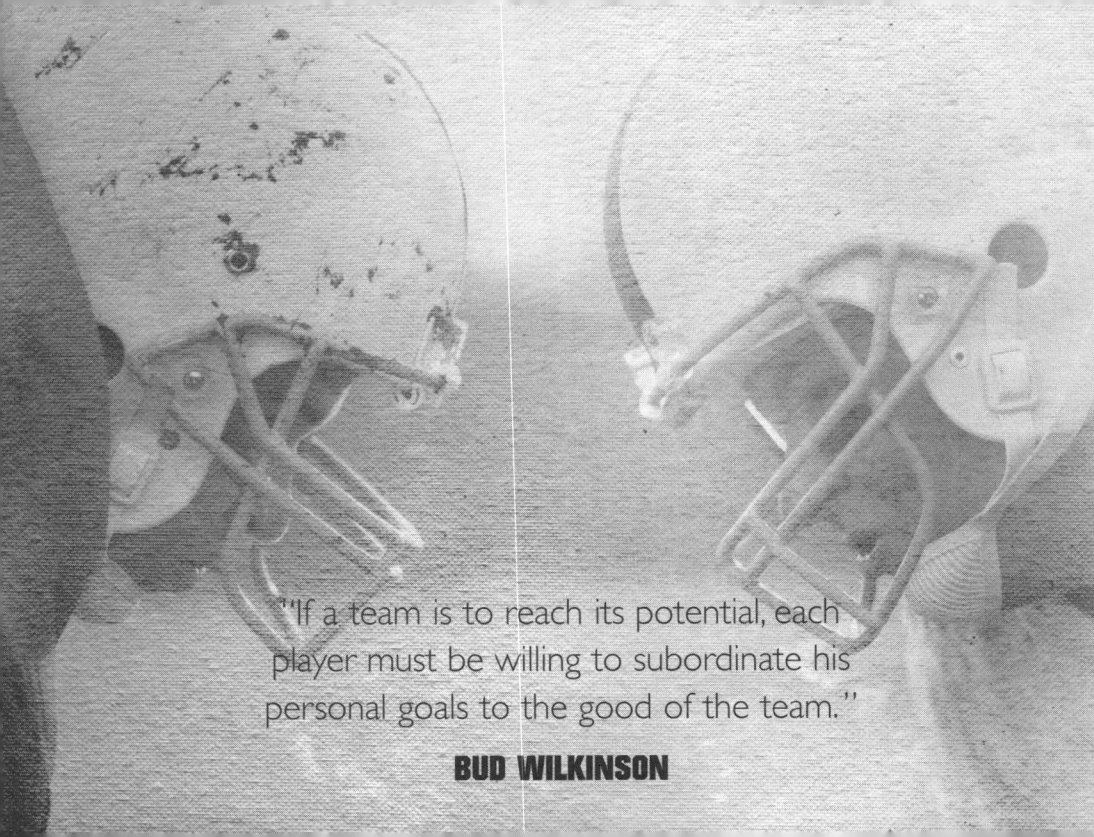

"If a team is to reach its potential, each player must be willing to subordinate his personal goals to the good of the team."

BUD WILKINSON

"God has commissioned us to run the race to win. He hasn't called us to shrink back and lie down. He hasn't called us to not hit them hard. He's called us to give it all we've got for His glory."

DARRELL GREEN

◆ ◆ ◆

"Franco Harris faked me out so bad one time that I got a 15-yard penalty for grabbing my own face mask."

D. D. LEWIS

*"The greatest quarterback is the guy who can make something happen.
He isn't necessarily the guy who can throw the tightest spiral."*

JOHN BRODIE

◆ ◆ ◆

"You can achieve only that which you will do."

GEORGE HALAS

◆ ◆ ◆

"Attitude is not just the way you think—it's the way you live."

YIELDING YOST

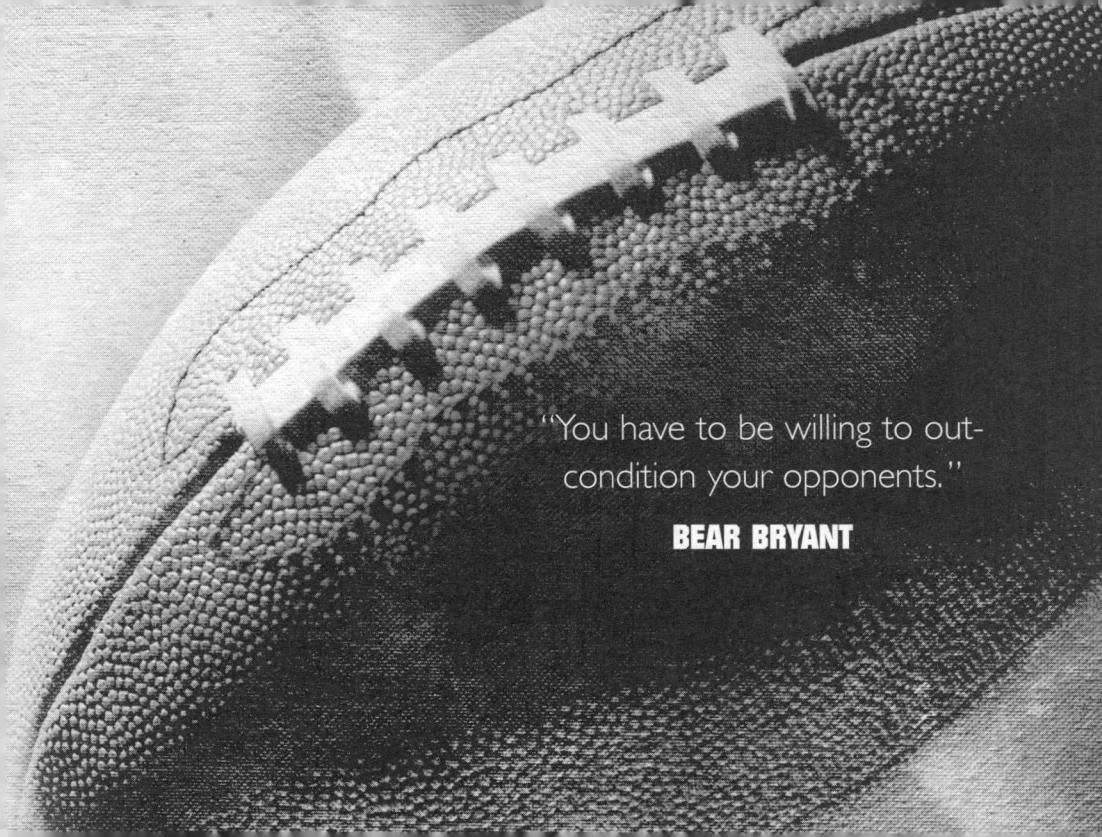

"You have to be willing to out-condition your opponents."

BEAR BRYANT

"Build your empire on the firm foundation of the fundamentals."
LOU HOLTZ

"When I hit a guy, I wanted him to know who hit him without his even having to look around and check a number."

DICK BUTKUS

◆ ◆ ◆

"I'm never satisfied with my performance because I know I can do better. I can help the team much more than I'm helping them. Not for self-gratification, but I can help the team."

DEION SANDERS

"Most people have their ligaments and cartilage inside their knees. I keep mine on the top of my locker."

JOE NAMATH

❖ ❖ ❖

"Inches make a champion, and the champion makes his own luck."

RED BLAIK

❖ ❖ ❖

"The most successful coaches on any level teach the fundamentals."

JOHN McKAY

"*Egotism is the anesthetic that dulls the pain of stupidity.*"

FRANK LEAHY

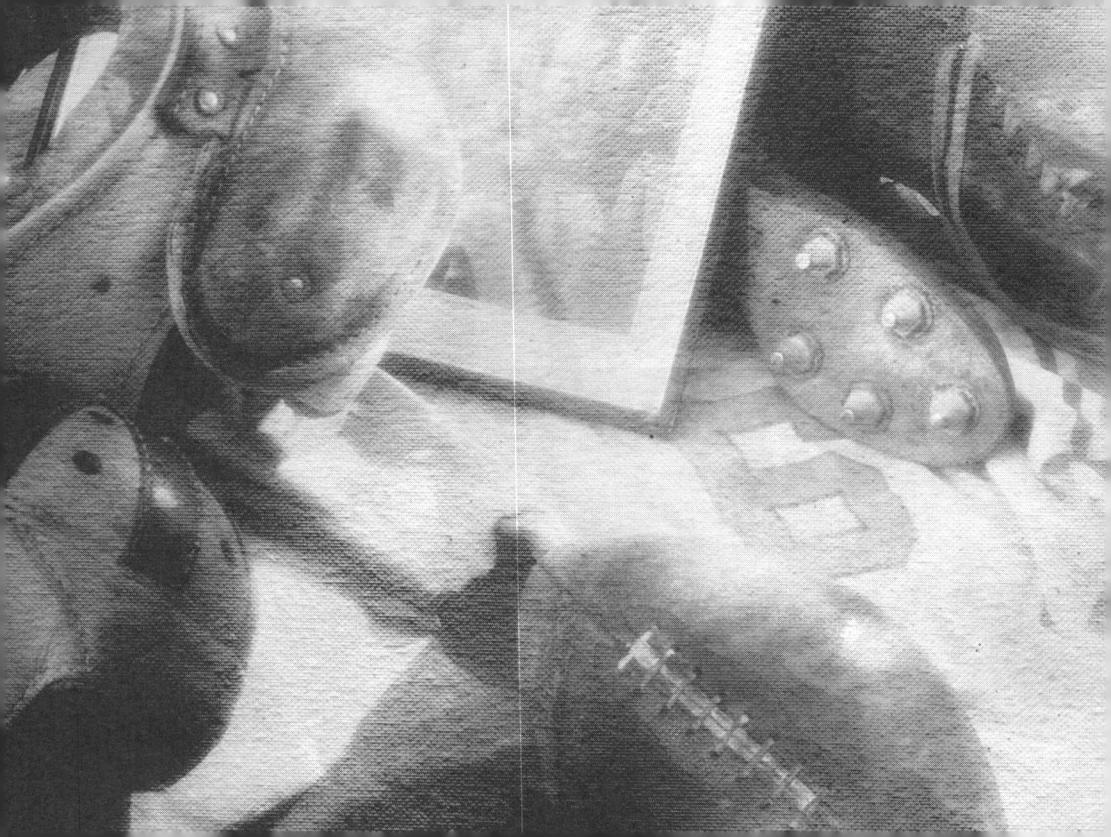

"It takes a lot of determination…a lot of stick-to-it-iveness. You have to want to enthusiastically do what you do and repeat what you do, day after day after day, if you're going to excel. We're all given gifts. What we do with the gifts that God has given us is our responsibility. You will fail. You will make mistakes. It's how you respond to your failures that really helps you to be successful."

JOHN KASAY

◆ ◆ ◆

"The secret to winning is constant, consistent management."

TOM LANDRY

◆ ◆ ◆

"In truth, I've never known a man worth his salt who, deep down in his heart, didn't appreciate discipline."

VINCE LOMBARDI

"Playing middle linebacker is like walking through a lion's cage in a three-piece pork-chop suit."

CECIL JOHNSON

◆ ◆ ◆

"It has to be very clear to the team who the coach is. I believe in that. Yet at the same time, the football players get it done. It's their team. The players should receive all the credit."

MIKE HOLMGREN

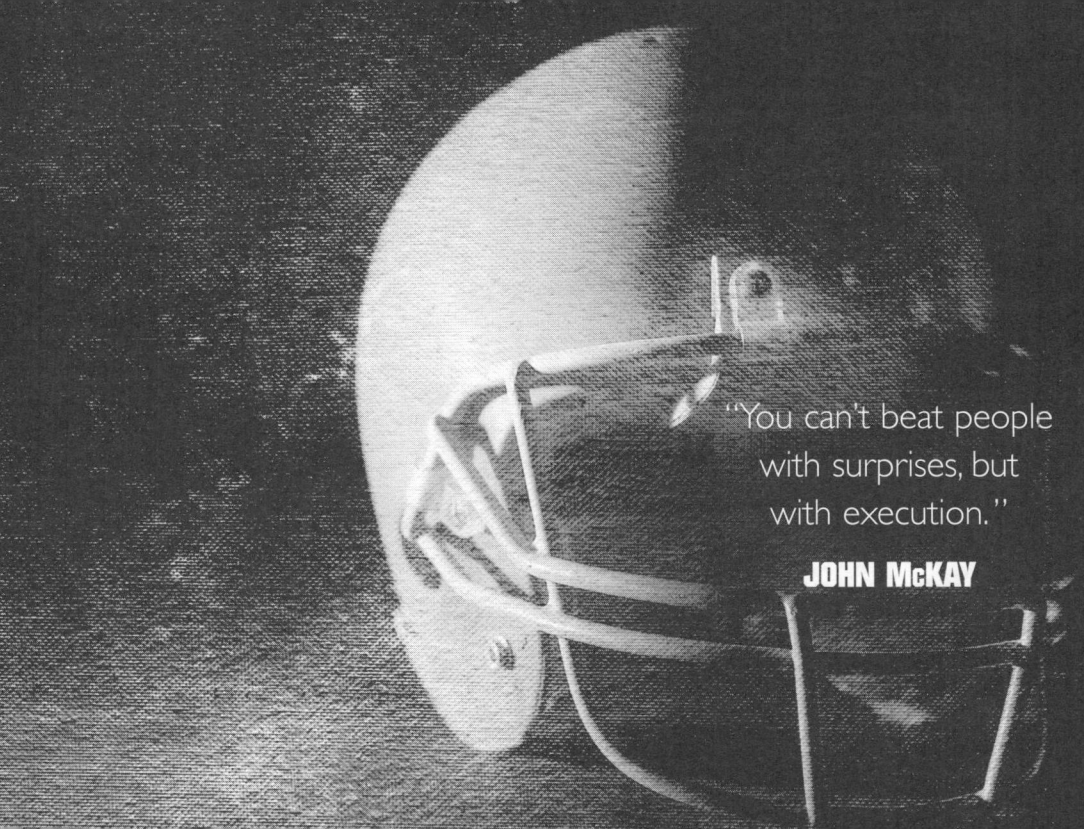

"You can't beat people
with surprises, but
with execution."

JOHN McKAY

"I never believed a boy was too small. You can't have too many good players. Good players win games, not big players."

LYNN "PAPPY" WALDORF

◆ ◆ ◆

"If a fellow makes a good hit on me, I'll pat him on the rear and say 'nice tackle.' But I'll be back."

GAYLE SAYERS

◆ ◆ ◆

"Difficulties in life are intended to make us better, not bitter."

DAN REEVES

"To be a successful coach in the NFL you have to be able to respond to trials and adversity. There's not a lot of positives in losing, but as long as you are learning from it, as long as you don't make the same mistakes twice and you're growing as you go, that's what you have to look at."

TONY DUNGY

◆ ◆ ◆

"You can motivate players better with kind words than you can with a whip."

BUD WILKINSON

◆ ◆ ◆

"Lombardi was a cruel, kind, tough, gentle, miserable, wonderful man whom I often hate and often love and always respect."

JERRY KRAMER

"Never let hope elude you.
That is life's biggest fumble."

BOB ZUPPKE

*"First, I prepare.
Then I have faith."*

JOE NAMATH

"Each of us has been put on earth with the ability to do something well. We cheat ourselves and the world if we don't use that ability as best we can."

GEORGE ALLEN

◆ ◆ ◆

"Nobody is going to wind you up every morning and give you a pep talk. So be a self-starter."

LOU HOLTZ

◆ ◆ ◆

"Catching passes is mostly a matter of getting the jump on the other guy. When you get the jump, size doesn't matter."

TOMMY McDONALD

"Only one thing is worse than going into a game thinking you can't win. That's going in convinced you can't lose."

BERNIE BIERMAN

◆ ◆ ◆

"I've always believed the greatest form of leadership is through example. You don't talk it, you walk it. You live it."

BART STARR

◆ ◆ ◆

"The quality of a man's life is in direct proportion to his commitment to excellence, regardless of his chosen field of endeavor."

VINCE LOMBARDI

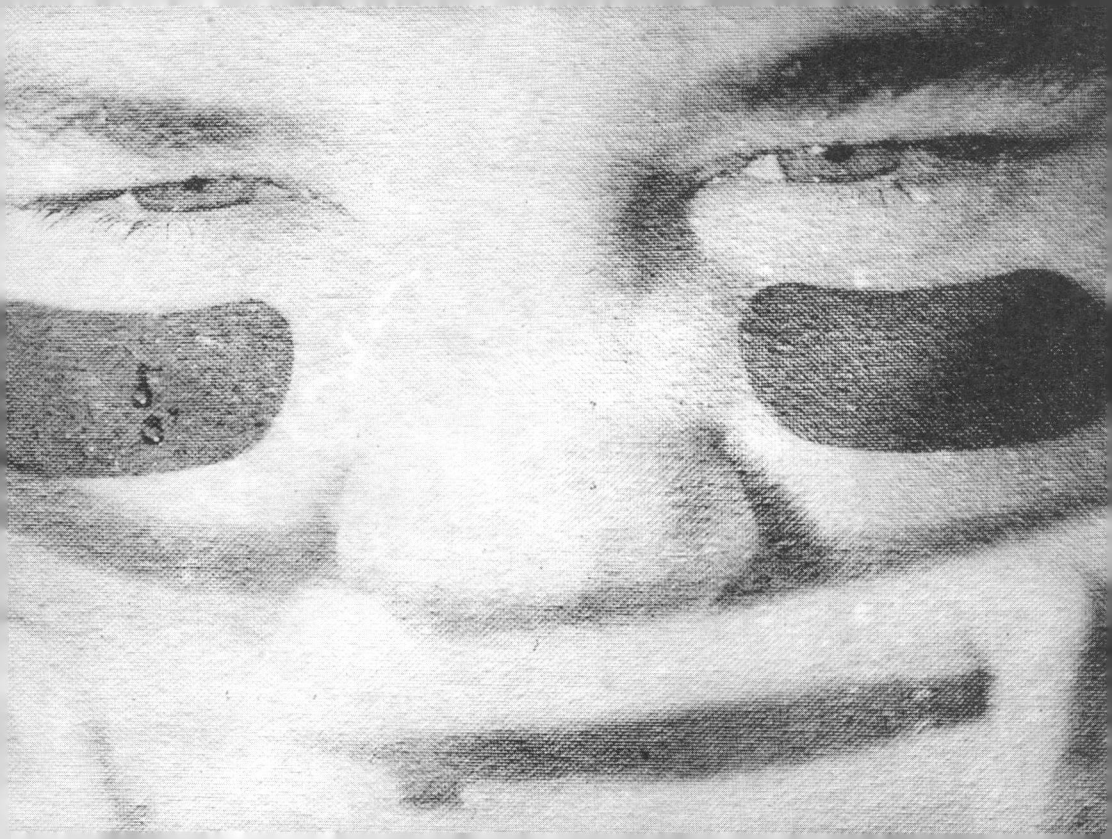

"I pray not for victory,
but to do my best."

AMOS ALONZO STAGG

"I love pressure. I thrive on it. When people expect me to do well, I expect myself to do twice as well as they expect me to do."

RANDALL CUNNINGHAM

◆ ◆ ◆

"Football is more mental than physical, no matter how it looks from the stands."

RAY NITSCHKE

◆ ◆ ◆

"There's only one bright side of losing—the phone doesn't ring as much the following week."

LOU HOLTZ

"Football is very temporary. You can't put your faith in something that can end so soon. I know that when I am on the field, God is with me. I count on Him to take care of me, to look after me, to protect me, and lead me in the right direction. When the pressure is on, I know He is standing right there next to me. Knowing that makes the game more enjoyable."

MARK BRUNELL

◆ ◆ ◆

"It's amazing how little difference there is between a winning effort and a losing one."

NORM SNEAD

"You cannot win if you cannot run."
HANK STRAM

"They say losing builds character. I have all the character I need."

RAY MALAVASI

"I've always believed in myself. I've always believed that I had the talent to get to this level and to be successful. I was just waiting for the opportunity. I was waiting for that door to open, to get a chance to prove to everybody that I could do it."

KURT WARNER

◆ ◆ ◆

"One guy can't do it by himself, and it's a matter of recognizing this and giving others their share of the credit."

ARCHIE MANNING

"Do what's right. Do your best. And treat other people like they want to be treated."

LOU HOLTZ

◆ ◆ ◆

"Most of my clichés aren't original."

CHUCK KNOX

◆ ◆ ◆

"Morale and attitude are the fundamental ingredients to success."

BUD WILKINSON

"Luck is what happens when preparation meets opportunity."

DARRELL ROYAL

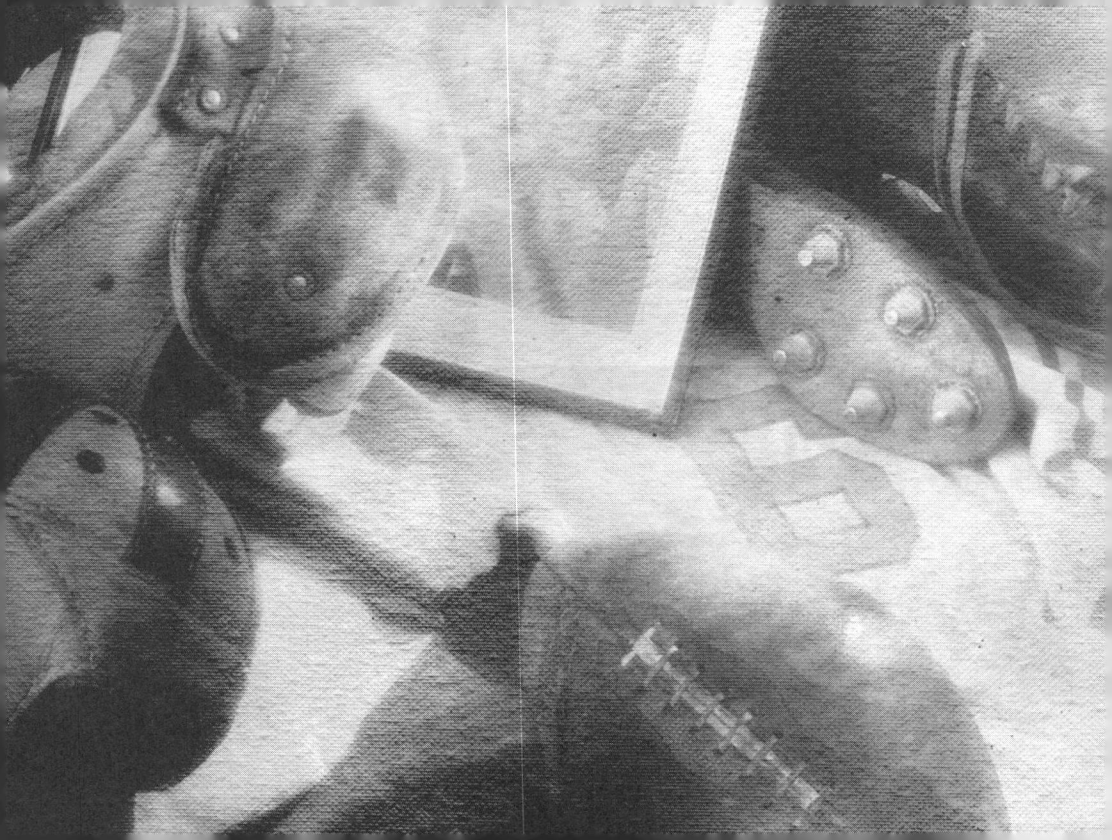

"Football is a great deal like life. It demands a man's personal commitment toward excellence and toward victory, even though he knows that ultimate victory can never be completely won."

VINCE LOMBARDI

◆ ◆ ◆

"If you hate your job, don't worry. You won't have it long."

GEORGE ALLEN

◆ ◆ ◆

*"You have to be respectful when arguing with an official.
I usually say, 'Sir, are we watching the same game?'"*

HOMER SMITH

"My idea of success is to know that I could play for anybody and have the respect around the league of other players and coaches. This, I think I accomplished."

BRIAN PICCOLO

◆ ◆ ◆

"The biggest thing I've learned is that the Lord has a plan for me. We don't always know what that plan is going to be or how we're going to get to where He wants us to be, but I've learned about perseverance. I've learned about being humble and being able to enjoy everything you get. I've grown. I've become a better player and a better person through the experiences I've had. To be starting in the Super Bowl and to have won the MVP is stuff you only dream about."

KURT WARNER

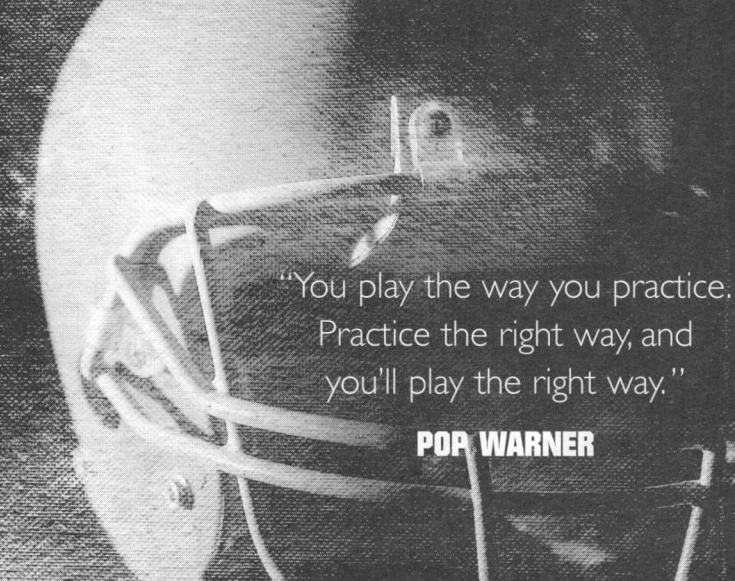

"You play the way you practice. Practice the right way, and you'll play the right way."

POP WARNER

"Hit the ball carrier harder than he hits you."

RAY NITSCHKE

"God didn't put me on the earth just to run up and down the football field."

DEION SANDERS

◆ ◆ ◆

"Believe deep down in your heart that you're destined to do great things."

JOE PATERNO

◆ ◆ ◆

"Nobody wants to follow somebody who doesn't know where he's going."

JOE NAMATH

"Football is an astonishing profession. It has enabled me to go from being an obscure member of the junior varsity at Harvard to becoming an honorary member of the Football Hall of Fame."

PRESIDENT JOHN F. KENNEDY

———————◆ ◆ ◆———————

"There never was a champion who to himself was a good loser. There's a vast difference between a good sport and a good loser."

RED BLAIK

*"Learn from everyone;
copy no one."*

DON SHULA

"The big players have got to come out and
make the big plays in the big games."

DEION SANDERS

◆ ◆ ◆

*In life, you'll have your back against the wall many times.
You might as well get used to it.*

BEAR BRYANT

◆ ◆ ◆

"Everybody is looking for instant success, but it doesn't work
that way. You build a successful life one day at a time."

LOU HOLTZ

*"In life, as in a football game, the principle to follow is:
hit the line hard; don't foul and don't shirk,
but hit the line hard."*

TEDDY ROOSEVELT

❖ ❖ ❖

"Success without honor is an unseasoned dish."

JOE PATERNO

❖ ❖ ❖

"Don't go to your grave with a life unused."

BOBBY BOWDEN

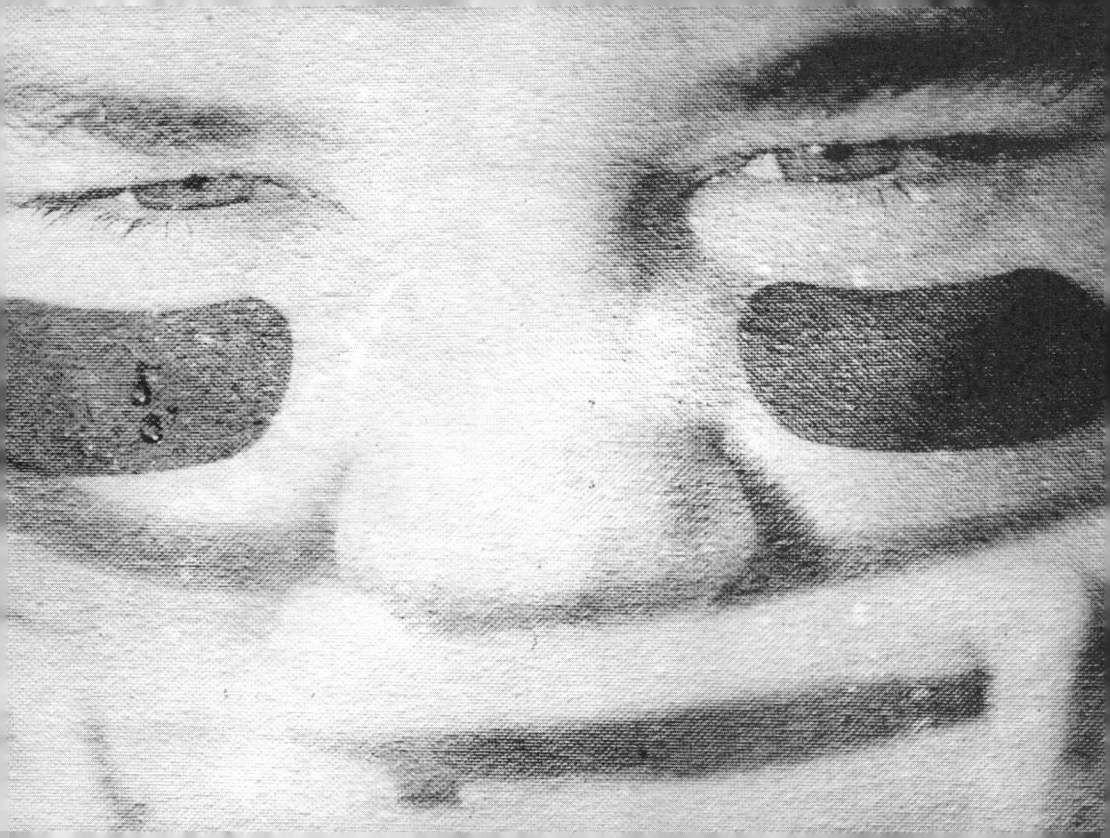

"It's good to have a lineman you can look straight in the belly button."

LARRY CSONKA

"When you think about Jesus' life on earth and what He did for us, it's the most beautiful thing that ever happened. And there are no strings attached."

MIKE HOLMGREN

◆ ◆ ◆

"There is something in good men that really yearns for discipline and the harsh reality of head-to-head combat."

VINCE LOMBARDI

◆ ◆ ◆

"Sure, luck means a lot in football. Not having a good quarterback is bad luck."

DON SHULA

"The greatest accomplishments occur, not when you do something for yourself, but when you do something for other people."

RONNIE LOTT

◆ ◆ ◆

"There's much more to playing quarterback than a strong arm, quick feet, or great reflexes. Without the right approach to the game, talent means nothing."

KEN ANDERSON

"First we will be best,
then we will be first."

LOU HOLTZ

"It's so easy to say, 'This is my body. This is my talent.' I'm smart enough to realize it is a gift from God, and it could have been given to somebody else. But it was given to me."

MIKE SINGLETARY

———— ◆ ◆ ◆ ————

"If your whole state of happiness comes from winning Super Bowls, you're going to be unhappy a lot of the time."

TROY AIKMAN

———— ◆ ◆ ◆ ————

"I've always considered myself a group therapist for 60,000 people. Every Sunday I held group therapy and the people came to take out their frustrations on me."

SONNY JURGENSEN

"I have no magic formula. The only way
I know to win is through hard work."

DON SHULA

◆ ◆ ◆

*"What defines the heart of a champion is the desire to
give your all and have no regrets about what you left
behind. The Bible doesn't say run the race so that you
achieve the crown. It says run the race in such a
manner that you would achieve the crown."*

JOHN MICHELS

"Winning is never final,
so bring on next season."

BILL PARCELLS

"When in doubt, punt."

BILL PETERSON

"When you find your opponent's
weak spot, hammer it."

JOHN HEISMAN

◆ ◆ ◆

*"For every pass I ever caught in a game,
I caught a thousand in practice."*

DON HUSTON

◆ ◆ ◆

"The way to succeed at quarterback
is to call the unexpected consistently."

JOHN HADL

"The Bible says that 'a good name is better to have than great riches.' I would rather have the good name that comes from being a godly man than to be in the Hall of Fame or have all the money in the world."

REGGIE WHITE

◆ ◆ ◆

"Play with small hurts."

VINCE LOMBARDI

◆ ◆ ◆

"I find that prayers work best when you have big players."

KNUTE ROCKNE

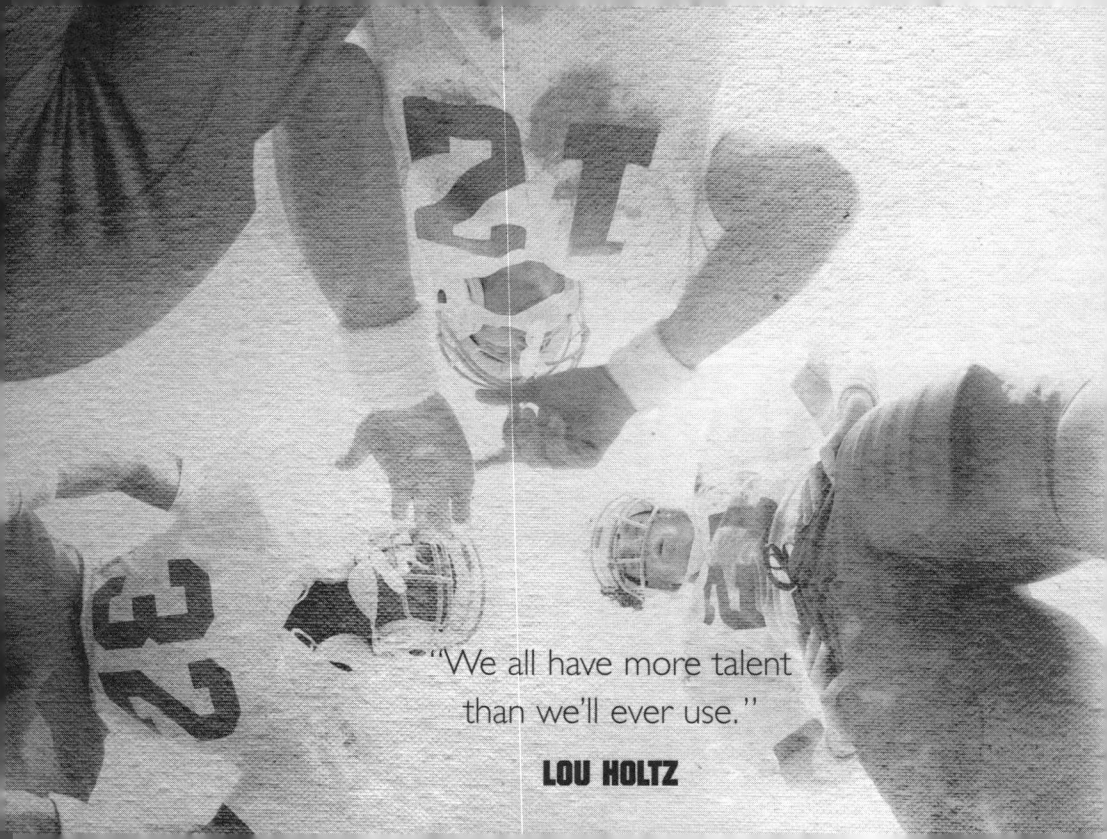

"We all have more talent
than we'll ever use."

LOU HOLTZ

"A champion is a person who has a soft heart. Soft in being understanding, honest, faithful, courteous, forgiving, and loving. But at the same time, it means being tough enough to go through the rough times, to be strong when you need to be strong."

IRVING FRYAR

◆ ◆ ◆

"You have to know when and how to go down. The key is to have a fervent desire to be in on the next play."

JIM ZORN

"Playing cornerback is like being on an island— people can see you but they can't help you."

EDDIE LEWIS

◆ ◆ ◆

"Look for players with character and ability. But remember, character comes first."

JOE GIBBS

◆ ◆ ◆

"Spectacular achievements are always preceded by unspectacular preparation."

ROGER STAUBACH

"There is no economy
in buying cheap equipment.
Buy only the best."

KNUTE ROCKNE

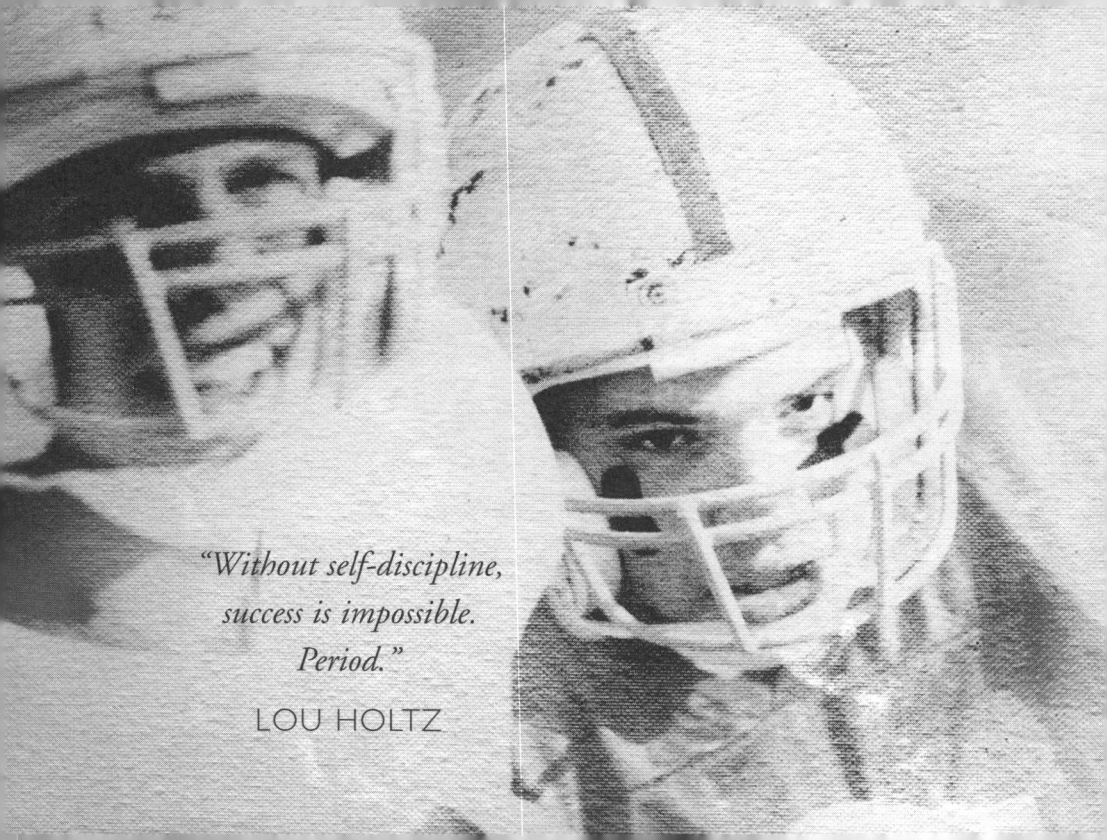

"*Without self-discipline, success is impossible. Period.*"
LOU HOLTZ

"Describing Don Shula as intense is like describing the universe as fairly large."

DAVE BARRY

◆ ◆ ◆

"God is bigger than a football game, and He wants to touch people's lives. That's what my goal is, and this gives me a platform."

KURT WARNER

"The achiever is the only individual who is truly alive.
I see no difference in a chair and the man who sits in
the chair, unless he's accomplishing something."

GEORGE ALLEN

◆ ◆ ◆

*"Give Emmitt Smith just a crease and he's something special.
He can stop on a dime and give nine and a half cents change."*

NATE NEWTON

◆ ◆ ◆

"In great attempts, it is glorious even to fail."

VINCE LOMBARDI

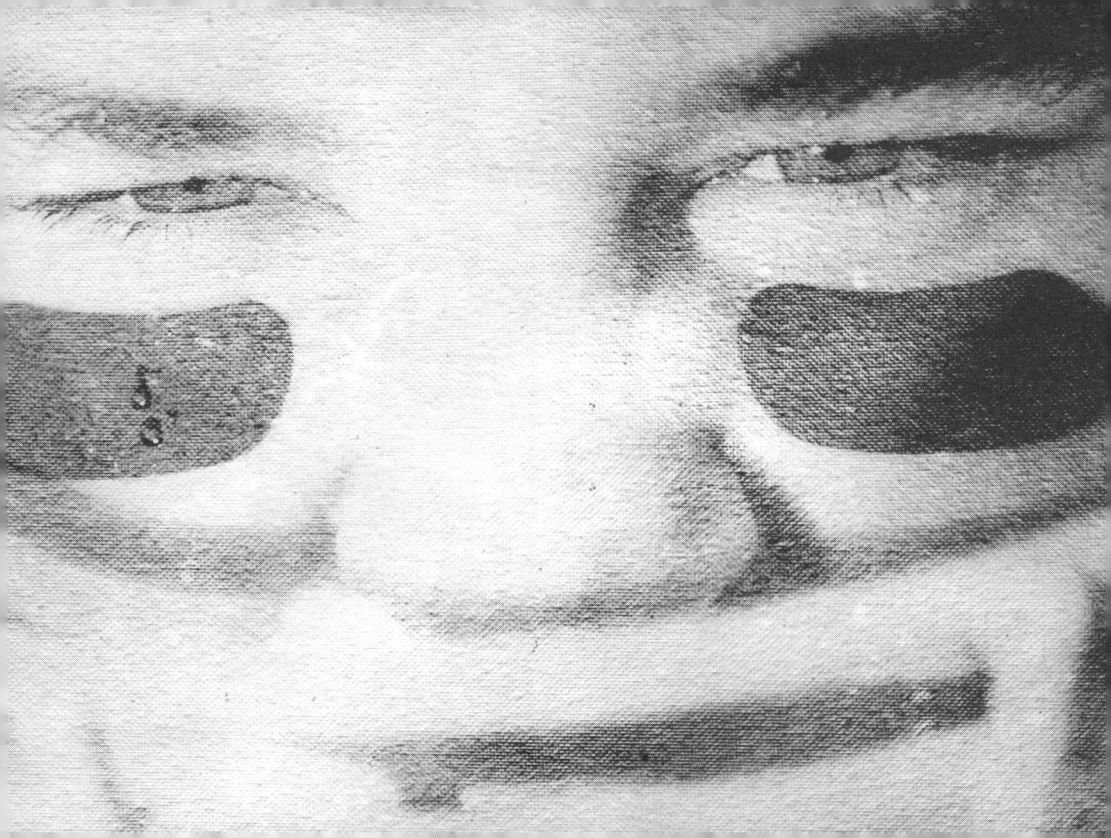

"I was a running back drafted by the Chicago Bears in the same year as Gale Sayers. Talk about being at the right place at the wrong time!"

BRIAN PICCOLO

◆ ◆ ◆

"Success is based on what the team does, not how you look."

KNUTE ROCKNE

◆ ◆ ◆

"Football, in its purest form, remains a physical fight. As in any fight, if you don't want to fight, it's impossible to win."

BUD WILKINSON

"In the NFL, there are 25 guys who can throw better than I can. But I can make guys win."

KEN STABLER

◆ ◆ ◆

"Winning is the science of being totally prepared."

GEORGE ALLEN

◆ ◆ ◆

"When God created a running back, he created Walter Payton."

JOHNNY ROLAND

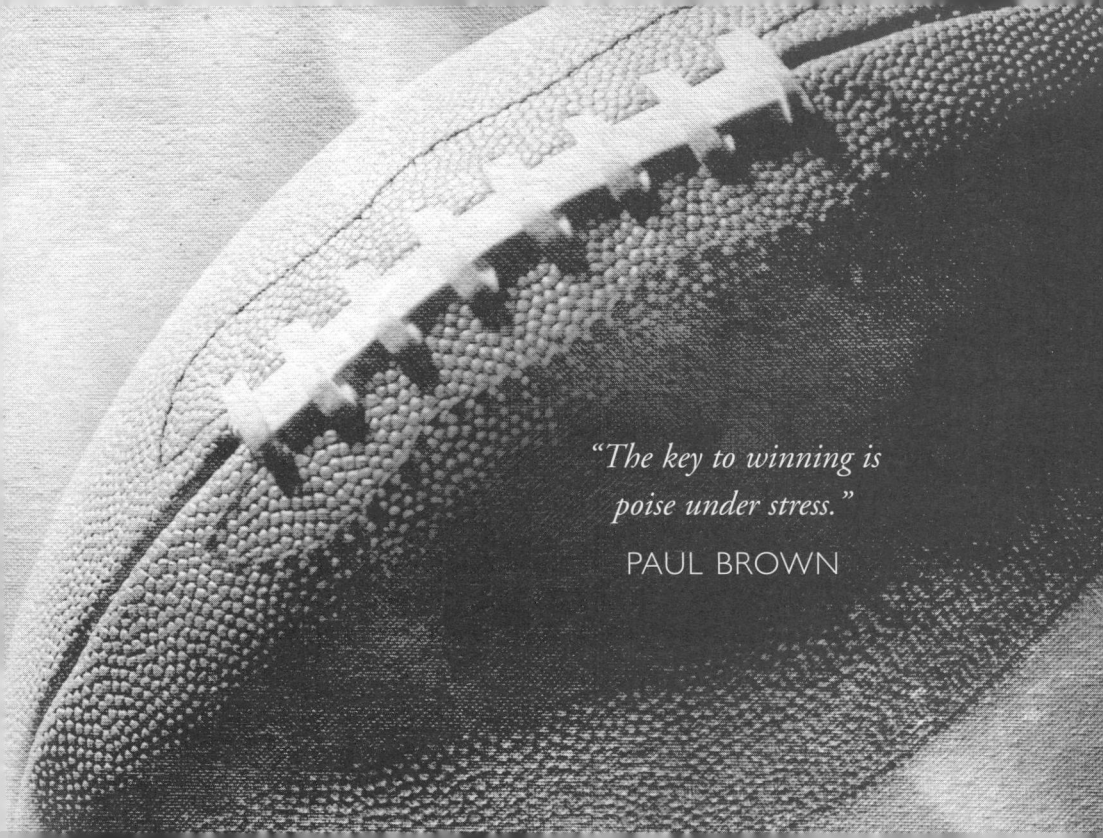

"The key to winning is poise under stress."

PAUL BROWN

"Nobody who ever gave his best regretted it."

GEORGE HALAS

◆ ◆ ◆

*"It doesn't matter how big or tall or wide you are.
It has to do with your desire and ability."*

BARRY SANDERS

◆ ◆ ◆

"Man's finest hour is the moment when he has
worked his heart out in a good cause and lies
exhausted on the field of battle—victorious."

VINCE LOMBARDI

"You lose games and you're 0 and 5, and you start thinking you're the first guy to get fired and have never won a game! But the great thing about being a Christian and knowing that God is in charge is to know I was going through that for a purpose. I think adversity can make you even better and propel you for years in the future. I think 0 and 5 did that for our football team, and I think we won some Super Bowls because of it."

JOE GIBBS

◆ ◆ ◆

"The only important thing about time of possession is who gets to keep the ball after the game is over."

LOU HOLTZ

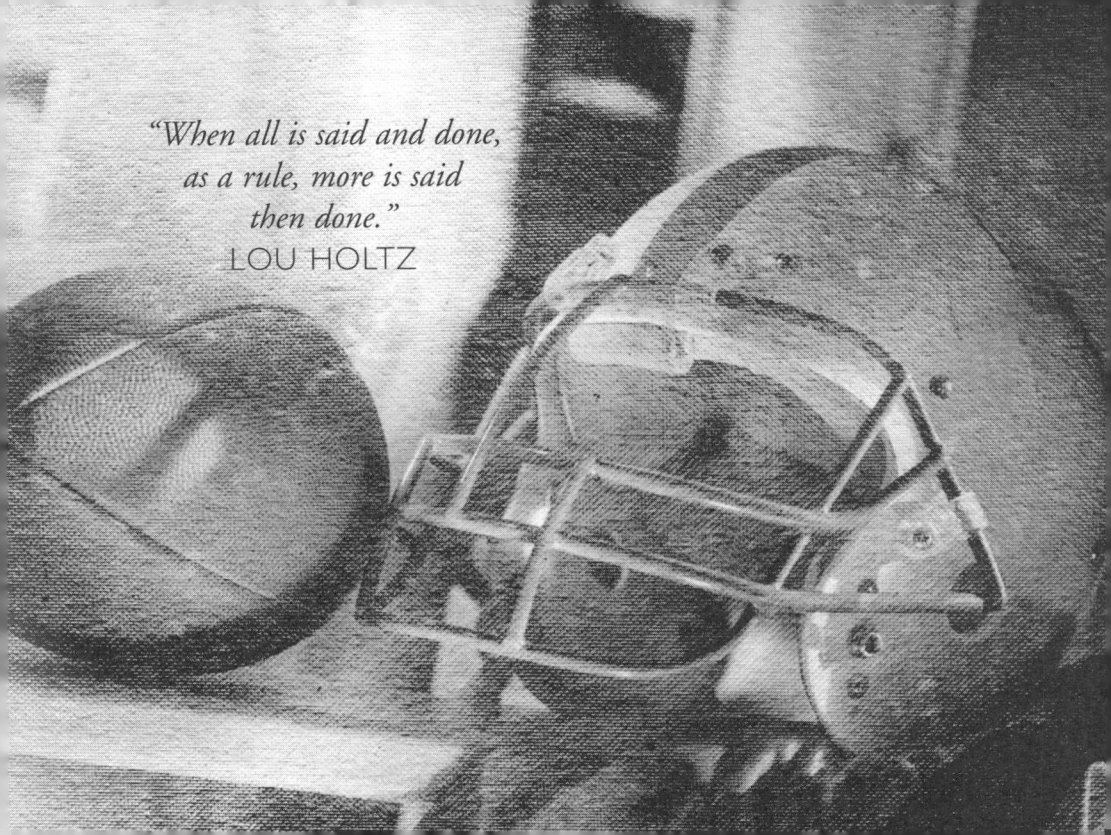

"When all is said and done, as a rule, more is said then done."
LOU HOLTZ

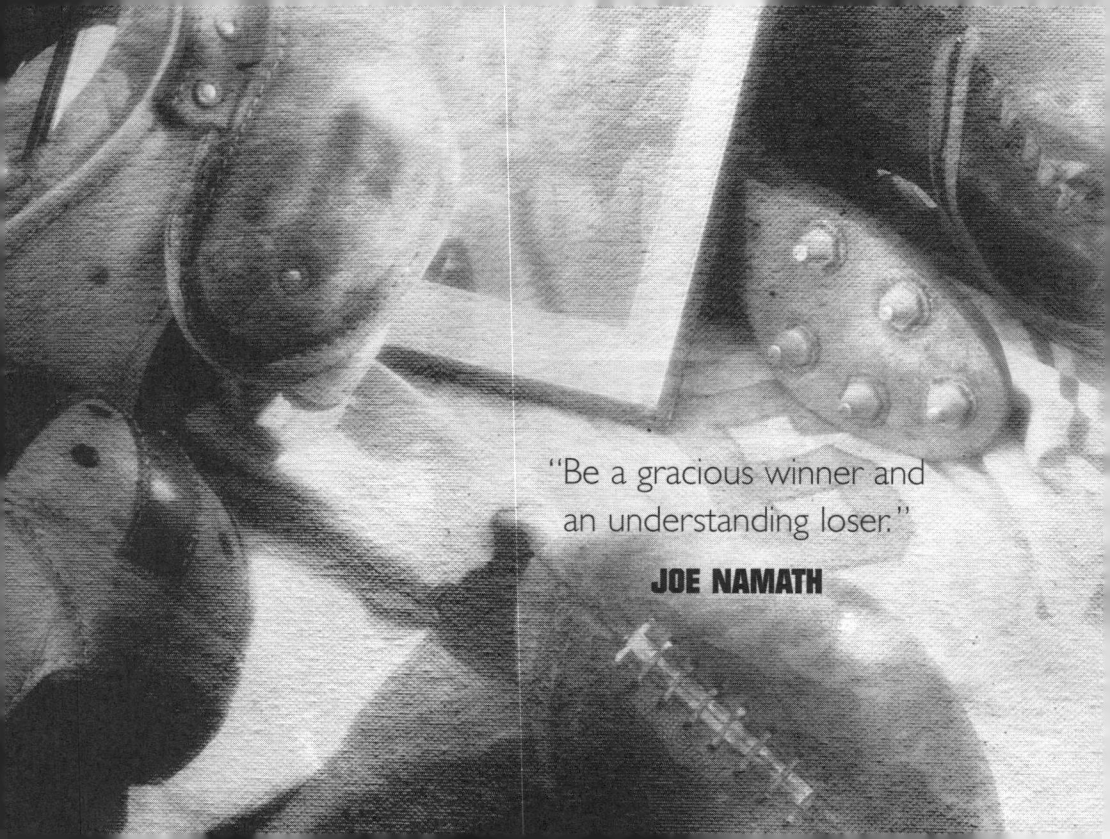

"Be a gracious winner and an understanding loser."

JOE NAMATH

"The great teams intimidate.
Not physically—psychologically."

JIM FINKS

◆ ◆ ◆

"I think we had the courage of David.
We just didn't have the skills of David."

LOU TEPPER

◆ ◆ ◆

"I've lost enough weight at various times
to put together an entire Little League team."

BUBBA PARIS

"All the height, strength, and speed in the world can be neutralized if the guy across from you gets a jump on the ball."

GEORGE PERLES

◆ ◆ ◆

"We compete, not so much against an opponent, but against ourselves. The real test is this: Did I make my best effort on every play?"

BUD WILKINSON

"Confidence is contagious.
So is the lack of confidence."

VINCE LOMBARDI

"The price for victory is hard work."

KNUTE ROCKNE

"If you want to catch more fish, use more hooks."

GEORGE ALLEN

◆ ◆ ◆

"The road to Easy Street goes through the sewer."

JOHN MADDEN

◆ ◆ ◆

"Assert your dignity."

JIM BROWN

"There isn't anything wrong with winning ugly. As a matter of fact, there isn't anything wrong with being ugly—as long as you're successful."

LOU HOLTZ

◆ ◆ ◆

"Why is football my kind of game? Because it tells you something about the character and intensity of the people who play it."

DICK VERMEIL

"Beat your opponent where he is strongest, and you demoralize him."

VINCE LOMBARDI

"Winning isn't everything,
but wanting to win is."

VINCE LOMBARDI

*"Winning is like shaving—you do it every day
or you wind up looking like a bum."*

JACK KEMP

◆ ◆ ◆

"You can be anything you want—
if you're willing to pay the price."

EDDIE ROBINSON

◆ ◆ ◆

*"The best thing I've learned in life is that things
have to be worked for. There's no magic in making
a winning team, but there's plenty of work."*

KNUTE ROCKNE

LANCE WUBBELS is the Vice President of Literary Acquisition and Development at Bronze Bow Publishing. He has authored several fiction and non-fiction books, including two of Hallmark's bestselling gift books, *If Only I Knew* and *Dance While You Can*. He has also written the Angel Award-winning novel *One Small Miracle* and the Gold Medallion-winning books *To a Child Love Is Spelled T-I-M-E* and *In His Presence*. And he has compiled and edited twenty-five other books that are published under his name.

TOM LEHMAN

A Passion
FOR
THE GAME

with Lance Wubbels. paintings by Donny Finley

A lifetime sports junkie, Wubbels considers working with Tom Lehman in the writing of *A Passion for the Game* to be a highlight of his literary career. Go to **www.TomLehman.com** and take a look at one of the most beautiful golf books ever published.

TO A CHILD LOVE
IS SPELLED
time

what a child *really needs from you*

MAC ANDERSON & LANCE WUBBELS

The heartwarming video for *To a Child Love Is Spelled T-I-M-E* has been sweeping through the Internet. Visit **www.BronzeBowInspiration.com** to view it and find more excellent gift books for every occasion.

UNLEASH *Your* GREATNESS

AT BRONZE BOW PUBLISHING WE ARE COMMITTED to helping you achieve your ultimate potential in functional athletic strength, fitness, natural muscular development, and all-around superb health and youthfulness.

Our books, videos, newsletters, Web sites, and training seminars will bring you the very latest in scientifically validated information that has been carefully extracted and compiled from leading scientific, medical, health, nutritional, and fitness journals worldwide.

Our goal is to empower you! To arm you with the best possible knowledge in all facets of strength and personal development so that you can make the right choices that are appropriate for *you*.

Now, as always, **the difference between greatness and mediocrity** begins with a choice. It is said that knowledge is power. But that statement is a half truth. Knowledge is power only when it has been tested, proven, and applied to your life. At that point knowledge becomes wisdom, and in wisdom there truly is *power*. The power to help you choose wisely.

So join us as we bring you the finest in health-building information and natural strength-training strategies to help you reach your ultimate potential.

FOR INFORMATION ON ALL OUR EXCITING NEW SPORTS AND FITNESS PRODUCTS, CONTACT:

BRONZE BOW PUBLISHING

2600 East 26th Street, Minneapolis, MN 55406
Toll Free: 866.724.8200
www.bronzebowpublishing.com